1981

From the creator of
THE COLLEGE SURVIVAL KIT

"In discussions of *The College Survival Kit*,
one statement always comes up:
I wish I had this book when I was in college!
Remembering back to those first frustrating
months of freshman year, I can understand
how almost everyone has trouble adjusting.

"Use this book often. Bone up from
time to time to make sure you're applying
its principles and methods of success.
It will always be of value to you."
—Irv Brechner

Educators and students endorse
THE COLLEGE SURVIVAL KIT

"A well-written 'first-aid kit'
for getting off to a great start."
—John C. Curry, Principal,
West Orange Mountain High School

"Should be required reading for all
college-bound students and for those students
who are presently floundering in college."
—Patrick G. Esposito, Principal,
East Hanover Middle School

"Written from a very
fresh, student's point of view."
—Alan L. Buechler, Director of Admissions,
Montclair State College

THE
COLLEGE
SURVIVAL
KIT

51 Survival Strategies

IRV BRECHNER

THE COLLEGE SURVIVAL KIT
A Bantam Book / August 1979

ISBN 0-553-01190-1

Published simultaneously in the United States and Canada

Bantam Books are published by Bantam Books, Inc. Its trademark,
consisting of the words "Bantam Books" and the por-
trayal of a bantam, is Registered in U.S. Patent and Trademark
Office and in other countries. Marca Registrada. Bantam
Books, Inc., 666 Fifth Avenue, New York, New York 10019.

PRINTED IN THE UNITED STATES OF AMERICA

0 9 8 7 6 5 4 3 2 1

Survival Strategies

Chapter One
ATTITUDE TOWARD COLLEGE   1

SS #1: What College Is . . .   4
SS #2: Why College Is Important   6
SS #3: Let's Talk About Finances   8
SS #4: Seven Basic Books Every College Student
       Should Have   10
SS #5: Class Attendance Is Necessary   13
SS #6: How Class Participation Helps Everyone   15
SS #7: Don't Put Off till Tomorrow . . .   16
SS #8: How to Have a Great Social Life at College 17
SS #9: How to Get the Most out of Homework   18

Chapter Two
PLANNING YOUR
FOUR YEARS AT COLLEGE   19

SS #10: How to Choose Your Courses and Professors 22
SS #11: How to Get the Most out of Your Professors 23
SS #12: Why You Should Know Your Advisors   25
SS #13: How to Vary Academic Loads   25
SS #14: How to Use Time Effectively   27
SS #15: Why You Should Make Dean's List   29
SS #16: What Other Honors You Can Achieve   29
SS #17: Why You Should Avoid Probation   30
SS #18: When to Study Overseas   31
SS #19: When to Consider Transferring or Exchange
        Programs   32
SS #20: How to Use Your College's Resources   34
SS #21: Why You Should Join Clubs   36
SS #22: What Are the Living Alternatives?   37
SS #23: How to Keep Your Body (and Mind) Healthy 40

Chapter Three
READING   43

SS #24: How to Time Your Reading   44
SS #25: What Is the Best Setting?   46

SS #26: How to Underline   47
SS #27: Taking Notes on Your Reading   49
SS #28: What Is the Best Attitude Toward Reading?   50
SS #29: How to Organize Your Reading   51
SS #30: How to Read Faster   52

Chapter Four
NOTE TAKING   53

SS #31: How to Organize Your Note Taking   55
SS #32: How to Set Up Your Notes   58

Chapter Five
WRITING PAPERS   61

SS #33: How to Organize Your Paper Writing   62
SS #34: How to Set Up Footnotes Properly   67
SS #35: How to Set Up Bibliographies Correctly   68
SS #36: Why Good Titles Are Necessary   69
SS #37: How Papers Are Graded   69

Chapter Six
EXAMINATIONS   71

SS #38: Be Prepared   72
SS #39: College vs. High-School Exams   73
SS #40: Forget About Curves and Scales   73
SS #41: Why You Shouldn't Cut Tests   74
SS #42: Different Types of Exams   74
SS #43: Midterms and Final Exams   80
SS #44: The New Method of Studying for Finals   81
SS #45: How to Master Take-Home Exams   82
SS #46: How Exams Are Weighed   83
SS #47: How Exams Are Graded   84
SS #48: An Option Called Pass/Fail   85
SS #49: How to Study for Tests   86
SS #50: Why You Should Never Cheat   88
SS #51: How to Find Out Where You Went Wrong   89

A Personal Note   90

1

ATTITUDE TOWARD COLLEGE

1

In the fall, campuses are again crowded with throngs of noisy students, weaving their way through the lively mobs toward the buildings and halls in which their futures will be molded in four quickly passing years.

Everyone usually comes to the first meeting of a class of the new term with new notebooks and pen in hand, talking about the past summer and expressing a readiness and eagerness to do well during the upcoming semester.

The class quiets down as the professor walks in, and many of the students give the instructor a close scrutiny with only one thing in mind: "Can I get an A or B from him? Will she flunk me? Does he grade on a curve?"

The professor, after collecting class cards and making a few introductory remarks, hands out a dittoed syllabus containing, along with office hours and course and section numbers, a list of required books and the respective readings for the term. Exclamations of surprise or more often disgust are uttered, depending on the length of the book list.

Since it is the first day of class, a majority of the profs generously dismiss their students early. The fresh-smelling purple dittos are shoved into notebooks and students race over to the bookstore to beat the mad rush for texts.

They consult their syllabi for the names and authors of books they need, and after locating them, wait on an endless line to pay. When their purchases are finally made, they are physically exhausted, sick of bookstores, and practically penniless.

When the semester is several days old the student has collected an impressive set of books, usually far more than the number of courses he's taking. Eventually, in the noisy "quiet" of a dormitory room, he glances over a course's reading requirements. After a reluctant addition, he sees that the readings come to over 500 tedious pages; this is a conservative estimate.

He also sees on the ditto the papers and/or exams he will be required to submit and/or take in order to complete the minimum course standards. He doesn't pay much attention to these facts since it is indeed the beginning, and "no one works in the beginning"; the syllabi become lost in a notebook, shoved in a crowded desk drawer, or tacked on a bulletin board behind flyers for the school football team or announcements of upcoming social events. These forgotten papers are usually not touched until a couple of days before exam time. Suddenly the student realizes he is swamped with work, and he remembers that hidden somewhere is his syllabus.

It is evident from these opening remarks that the attitudes of many students have fallen into a set pattern, inherited from some upperclassmen. Or the invitations of mother nature may prove to be too strong to resist, so athletics and dating take up a major part of the student's time. These patterns of behavior toward schoolwork, molded in most cases during the first few weeks of school, are largely responsible for poor progress in collegiate academics.

My purpose is to redirect the existing traditional modes of study acquired in high school that allow for endless free time with decidedly negative results into a productive, positive, result-oriented concept of study. I will suggest several techniques of study which can help a frustrated student gain a sense of accomplishment in the form of grades he desires or meeting the expectations of others. In addition, proper use of these hints will leave you with enough free time to really enjoy college life.

To be reasonably successful in your college endeavors, you must have a positive (not necessarily the most pleasing or ideal) attitude and disposition toward what you'll face while in college. There are several strategies which you should learn, in order to gain from college that which will solidify your future.

Survival Strategy #1:

What College Is . . .

First and foremost comes the realization that college usually is not what it is played up to be in high school. Instead of the many small classes college recruiters boast of, you will probably find that many college courses have more students than a high-school gym class.

Your eager anticipation of taking stimulating and unusual courses will fade away as you repeatedly come across two of the most dreaded words on your registration schedule: CLOSED OUT. Annoying problems crop up, as in every life situation, which tend to make the college experience a good primer for the "real" world.

Like every endeavor into which you put in an extra-special effort, college offers so much, and taking good advantage of these four years should be your goal.

The pressure in high school to gain acceptance at a good college or university continues in another form. The stress on grades remains the same as in high school—if not increased—due to the emphasis placed on an advanced degree, and the severe competition for the better-paying jobs that are available. Companies have their pick of graduates and usually concentrate on the top 10 percent of the class.

Another big difference between high school and college is the sheer quantity of work—there is three to six times as much work as in most high schools. In high school there was a daily schedule planned for you. There were teachers and parents to make sure your work was done. But college lectures are often optional and the freedom you so eagerly desire means there is no one to check up on you and push you. You have to push yourself!

Most professors assume that students are adults and will act in an adult manner—the profs won't lead anybody by the hand, but will be available to counsel you should a problem arise. The focus of the high-school teacher was on the pupil, while at college the professor concentrates for the most part of the subject being taught.

Don't decide that college is too tough for you before you start and that you won't be able to do as well as in high school. The difficulty of the work is not the problem. The proper use of *time* is the main obstacle which causes the collapse of many students. Most of the topics in this book, therefore, are *time-oriented*, so that you will be prepared for this aspect of college life.

Speaking of time, you've spent roughly 16,000 hours studying and attending school so far in your lifetime. Next come the 6,000 hours in college which are so very important to your future. Learning to budget your time is probably the most useful technique you will ever acquire.

Consequently, college probably will not turn out to be the breeze you may have pictured it to be while in high school.

Survival Strategy #2:

Why College Is Important

The emphasis in college, as in high school, is on getting the grades. Why? In high school the cream of the crop, those with the best grade achievements, are usually chosen by the best colleges. Those with lesser averages may wind up receiving lower quality higher education at a mediocre school.

After college graduation, the cream of the crop have a better chance of obtaining quality employment or getting into graduate schools. Those who didn't place enough emphasis on academics in college usually don't obtain the positions they desire. Entering the working ranks may seem like a long way off, but four years at college pass all too quickly.

The obvious conclusion is that you must realize the importance of college in relation to your future. Once this concept is embedded in your mind, the successive steps of "more work and less play" will be easier for you to accept.

It usually takes time, in some cases over two years, to adjust to college, its pressures and demands. The sooner you acquire a positive attitude toward learning within the system, the faster you will make the transition.

These arguments all lead to your placing work above all other activities—but, of course, not eliminating them. There will be plenty of time (if you don't waste it) for both. It calls for a will and ability to say no to friends' invites when an exam, a paper, or even important homework assignments have to be finished. *Your friends will still be around to socialize with after your work is done.*

Sure, this may sound like "all work and no play," but firsthand experience has found it to be a crucial part of success in college to place priority on work. You *will* have time left over for sports, dates, and other activities. The result is the education you need and an opportunity to participate in a wide variety of nonacademic programs and activities.

You will undoubtedly question the necessity of one or more of the many courses you'll take in college. You may say, when your mind is made up about your career goal, "I don't see how this course can help me." Many colleges urge and even require various courses so that their students can:

(1) grow in the ability to think and express themselves intellectually in many areas;

(2) become aware of the surrounding world outside the campus;

(3) appreciate cultural aspects such as art, music, and theater that one may not have previously been exposed to;

(4) become responsible in an organized society;

(5) choose and prepare for a vocation on a professional level.

The importance of some of these required courses will become clear after graduation.

Survival Strategy #3:
Let's Talk About Finances

From a financial point of view, one held by your parents, and in some cases by you, expenditures at a college are primarily for tuition and/or room and board—not for pleasure only, as some use it. A student who goes to college just to fool around certainly isn't getting his (or his parents') money's worth. Instead, in exchange for four years of fun and games, he is seriously hampering his future and all the joys it holds.

Now that you've decided not to cut classes because it is a waste of money, let's look at how and where to get financial aid if you need it.

Even if you think you don't have a chance at getting financial aid, you should visit the financial aid office on campus and look over their list of various scholarships, stipends, awards, grants, and special appropriations made possible by a tremendously varied group of sponsors.

Unknown to the general college population, there are many, many means of improving your financial situation while in college. Several service groups such as the Lions and the Elks give aid to sons and daughters of their members. Other ethnic and religious societies give scholarships to persons of merit belonging to their particular group.

On the federal and state levels there are government aid programs, usually administered by the college itself. Direct grants, national low-interest student loans, supplementary grants to students from low-income families, armed services programs, and veterans' benefits are also available. You can get direct state grants and state-guaranteed loans. There are also sources of financial assistance known as endowments, usually scholarship funds set up under the auspices of trusts, individuals, state and local organizations, and banks.

Details about all these aid programs are usually printed up by the college and can be obtained at the financial aid office. You may find an obvious or obscure way of getting that much needed aid.

If, after exhausting these avenues, money is still a problem, why not consider a part-time job? There are basically three categories:

- a job on campus at the library,
  cafeteria, etc., or one off campus at a

local store or company—check the placement office for listings

- a job or service which draws on specific skills you have: typing term papers, tutoring, writing articles of various kinds for local newspapers, etc.

- a related job in a college department, such as assistant to the marketing department or aide in the nursing school

The major consideration in deciding whether you have to work, besides the obvious financial situation, is your capability to handle college academics, a social and athletic life, and a job. In most cases, if time is used properly, 10 to 20 hours of work per week can be fitted into your schedule.

Survival Strategy #4:

Seven Basic Books
Every College Student Should Have

The following is a recommended list of the books you should always have on hand when you are studying. They will comprise the beginnings of your own reference library. I am only suggesting the specific titles given—they are excellent but not the only books available.

1. A good dictionary is an absolute must. You will refer to it for meanings, spelling, and syllabification. You'll want to keep a dictionary handy

when you're reading, so that you can look up the unknown words. (It will help your memory if you jot them down with corresponding definitions on a vocabulary list.) Three excellent dictionaries you might choose from are *Webster's New Collegiate Dictionary* (Merriam-Webster), *American Heritage Dictionary of the English Language* (McGraw-Hill), or *The Scribner-Bantam English Dictionary* (Scribner's). A paperback dictionary is nice to have to take to the library. You might choose *The Scribner-Bantam English Dictionary* (Bantam 1979), which is unabridged. Remember, a good dictionary is a good investment.

2. A thesaurus is also essential. You will use it often while writing. Its purpose is to give you synonyms—words that mean the same thing. When used properly, it can expand your vocabulary and stretch your mind. But be careful not to use the thesaurus without thinking through the choices it provides. The most widely used thesaurus is Roget's. One good edition is *Roget's International Thesaurus*, 4th edition (Crowell).

3. *The Elements of Style*, 3rd edition, W. Strunk, Jr. & E. B. White (Macmillan, hardcover and paperback). This small book (78 pages) provides a wealth of information on styling your writing. The author presents rules of usage, composition, and form in a clear manner. It has helped countless students over three decades and should be an invaluable aid to you throughout college and beyond.

4. *A Manual for Writers of Term Papers, Theses, and Dissertations*, 4th edition, Kate L. Turabian (University of Chicago Press, hardcover and paperback). This is also a style manual, aimed at

helping you organize your finished thoughts into a well-ordered piece of writing. The author explains how to use quotations, tables, documents, footnotes, and bibliographies.

5. *Writing and Researching Term Papers and Reports: A New Guide for Students*, Eugene Ehrlich & Daniel Murphy (Bantam, paperback). This is a guide to developing a term paper, from choosing a topic to reseaching and writing your paper. If used in conjunction with the previous two books, your papers are sure to be top-notch!

6. *Basic Grammar for Writing: A Step-by-Step Course in all the Essentials of Clear Writing*, Eugene Ehrlich & Daniel Murphy (McGraw-Hill, paperback). This book is exactly what its title says. Although you've already learned English grammar in elementary and high school, the purpose of having this book on hand is to be able to refer to it when you have a question about specific problems of grammar and usage.

7. A Bible is another essential—not necessarily for religious reasons, but as a reference tool. Your English, history, art, philosophy, and other professors will refer to sections of the Bible. If you don't know this book, chapter and verse, the references you come across will be wasted. Make a habit of looking them up to see their particular relevance. Any King James version with a concordance in the back will serve your needs.

Survival Strategy #5:

Class Attendance Is Necessary

The policies of colleges on the subject of class attendance are continually changing, but my experience indicates that attendance on a regular basis is a must. The joys of cutting class consistently (to sleep late or play frisbee) are soon forgotten, but the poor grades evidenced later are on record and will be remembered a lot longer.

Missing classes every once in a while for a good reason is usually OK, but the habitual class cutter cannot hope for good results.

The reasons for sustained class attendance are rather obvious, but should be emphasized here. The four basic factors which make attendance imperative are:

1. The format used by a majority of the professors in the presentation of their course material. The lecturing process results in two actions: written lecture material (notes) and oral understanding with some of the material remembered subconsciously. You can cut a class and later get the notes, but you will be missing an important element: your comprehension of what the prof said. By not being there, you may have missed an explanation or example which clarified a particular thought. This clarification may have been omitted from your friend's notes or may have been completely misunderstood by him.

2. Psychologists tell us that verbal memory (hearing) in many cases has proved to be better or at least highly complementary to written memory (notes). In other words, what may be missed in note

taking may be remembered either consciously or subconsciously and will be recalled later when needed. It is impossible to copy every word the prof says.

3. Questions pertaining to material just presented can be asked right then and there in class. Questions encountered while copying over someone else's notes will probably never be answered, for two reasons:

- the prof is not always around for help, especially the night before an exam

- you may not take the time to question a statement if you're not in class, especially if you're the type who cuts class in the first place.

4. Many professors take attendance, supposedly, just to see who's there, saying: "It doesn't count toward the final grade." But let's face it, a string of X's denoting excessive absenteeism will probably sway even the strongest-willed professor toward downgrading your grades.

There are four other factors to consider before cutting classes:

Yourself: Obviously if you are terrible at English, you won't want to miss any English classes. But if you're a math whiz, you may find you can miss more than once in a while.

Professor: Some profs require perfect attendance, while others don't care if you ever show up. Check out each prof's policy.

School: Some colleges have strict attendance rules—which are sometimes enforced.

Major: It's important to get superior grades in your major field of study. So don't cut classes in your major.

Survival Strategy #6:
How Class Participation Helps Everyone

Asking questions in class concerning material not understood often causes problems. If you are the type who gets embarrassed when asking questions in class, and consequently don't, look at it from this point of view: You are paying (or your parents are) a certain amount of money for your education, and you are entitled to additional help as well as explanations in class. If the prof refuses to give you help and answer questions, he is violating his employment contract. You are paying for this service, so use it!

Asking questions not only will benefit you in terms of the answer but provide the rest of the class with your individual insights. When other students ask questions, listen, and participate, you'll learn something from the many varied viewpoints present in the class. This group cohesiveness and open discussion will usually lead to a better understanding of the material, and give the professor an opportunity to observe the students' reaction to the material he's presented.

It is usually wise to sit in front or near the front of the class. Sitting up front improves your:

- hearing
- seeing

- eye contact with the prof
- attention span

Sit where you won't be talking and daydreaming. Socialize afterward and concentrate during class.

Survival Strategy #7:

Don't Put Off till Tomorrow . . .

One of the most common devices employed with nearly 100 percent efficiency by college students is bypassing work assignments through rationalization. Students convince themselves with seemingly logical but faulty arguments that their work can be postponed in order to have fun, and still get done.

I'm not saying you mustn't rationalize, for everyone does at one time or another. In justifying poor class attendance or not completing an assignment, rationalization should be kept at a minimum, to avoid a pile of work later on. A simple reason lies behind the theory of not letting too much work accumulate—the future. No one can predict the future. Work can pile up in two ways:

1. The prof can actually assign additional work (surprise!) to be completed in the near future.

2. With the same amount of work, special and unexpected activities can arise (homecoming) that no student should miss. But the work still has to be done.

Total abstention from rationalization may be impossible, but a prudent restriction of it is the least risky approach.

Survival Strategy #8:

How to Have a Great Social Life at College

At this point you're probably asking: "When do I have time for my social life?" When you've absorbed the procedures and techniques for scheduling your work as presented throughout *The College Survival Kit*, you'll know how and where to take advantage of free time for nonacademic purposes.

My college years were the best four years of my life, for I combined academics, dating, sports, and club activities, which gave me a well-rounded daily schedule.

It's important to remember that I'm not asking you to give up anything—just to rearrange your priorities and concept of time to make proper use of it.

Tying up the first eight survival strategies, we see that your attitude is probably the most important factor for your success in college. Saying "I'm gonna work hard this year" is not enough. Sacrifices that hurt must be made daily, or the result will be below-par employment after graduation.

The postgrad job field is limited to those qualified, and the only means to quantitatively judge a graduating senior is by that magical number, the cumulative average. And cums are determined, of course, by a combination of test scores, papers— and only in small part by subjective factors.

It must be unconditionally accepted that paper and exam grades are the most important factors in the prof's decision (in 99 percent of courses) about the final grade you'll receive. Though exams many times test "what you don't know," they're what counts, so it is better to learn how to study for them and do well than to try and change our particular system of learning and flunk out in the process. In spite of much experimenting, no solid, large-scale alternative to written exams has been found applicable to all fields of study.

Survival Strategy #9:
How to Get the Most out of Homework

The importance of homework depends on the course. Homework here is defined as *a written assignment*. If homework is to be handed in, it is obviously important to your grade.

It is important to do your homework for another, more important reason. The only way some material can be learned is by repetition of problems. Doing problem after problem, you become proficient. Remember, you learned how to add through continual practice, not by rote memory. Some courses in which homework is a necessity due to problems are accounting, biology, chemistry, computer science, economics, math, foreign languages, and physics. Homework is actually a preparation for the exam in most of these courses.

This is not to say that you don't have to do homework in other courses! Just as in attendance, concentrate on weak areas. *Remember, a homework assignment is not something you do for a prof; you do it for yourself.*

2
PLANNING YOUR FOUR YEARS AT COLLEGE

2

You don't generally go to college just to get good grades. There's a lot more involved—preparing for a career, enjoying the social and athletic events, becoming a member of one or more clubs, and having some good old fun too!

The first thing to do is look at and evaluate the situation you'll be in four years from now. Primarily you must decide, not necessarily on the exact career you want, but what your goals will look like at graduation time.

Many students aspire to a decent job with a good salary and benefits and nothing more. Others want mental stimulation, and do not place as much emphasis on financial reward. Still others are looking for that top money-making position in a corporation. Every student is different, but by now you should have, or begin to formulate, an idea of the type of career you'd like to have.

The first step, therefore, is to pinpoint your destination when you graduate. After establishing a goal, you can create a game plan by which you can get to that goal with as little aggravation and as much enjoyment as possible.

It would be a good idea to look into sources suggested by your librarian which describe the various jobs or professions you can eventually get into. For example, there are many different kinds of engineers: chemical, ceramic, electrical, civil, to list just a few. Choosing a broad field, and having several alternatives within it, will aid you in selecting an area of interest. But before you decide upon a major, you should take a broad variety of courses to expose yourself to the whole spectrum of available careers.

Suppose you've narrowed your interests and aptitudes to three areas. It is time to design your first year's courses, keeping in mind your goal and the school's requirements for graduation. Courses which must be taken in order to graduate should be completed as soon as possible, preferably in the first year. Along with two or three of these required courses, try to take one or two courses in each of the areas you're interested in.

By the end of your freshman year, one area will usually present itself as the most favorable, interesting, and probably the best choice for you. The beginning of the sophomore year can be the time to choose and declare your major. However, don't be alarmed if you don't firm up your major until the middle or end of the sophomore year—there is still time to complete the requirements for the major you choose.

We're at the point, two to four semesters into your college career, where you have made a tentative decision about your major. The next step is to consult with an advisor in your major department about requirements, career opportunities, and other advice you can gain. This is a most important meeting; choosing your major correctly and planning out the program is critical to the job you will end up with.

We will now outline the registration and course selection procedure, which has certain limitations when you're a freshman. Reading this section carefully will help you get the courses you're most interested in taking.

Survival Strategy #10:

How to Choose Your Courses and Professors

The procedures for deciding which courses to take are basically the same everywhere: they are left up to you, with guidance from advisors. Here are several things to keep in mind.

1. Always decide which courses to take far in advance (two to four weeks) of the actual registration date, if possible. Many courses have prerequisites: you must complete one course before you can take a more advanced one. Seats are usually given out on a seniority basis, so have alternates ready in case some of your first choices are closed out.

2. Between the time you choose your courses and registration, talk to friends, profs, advisors, and parents about your course selection. Most schools list the prof's name along with the section he'll be teaching. Find out what the prof is like—make sure, though, to get several opinions. Course and profes-

sor evaluation books are becoming available on some campuses. Consult if available.

3. Make up your schedule in advance to determine your specific sections and their time slots. Make sure there are no conflicts (two courses at the same time on the same day).

4. On registration day, make sure you have all information and alternate selections. If possible, get there early, so you will have a better chance to get all the courses you want.

5. After your program is approved, hold on to your schedule in case of a computer mishap. You should receive your class admittance cards as soon as your tuition bill is paid.

To summarize: Try to plan a program which will let you meet the university requirements and study in your specific area of interest, and be flexible enough to let you change your major should you lose interest. Try to take a variety of courses for the first two to three semesters, and then specialize—unless you are *absolutely* sure, from the start, of the direction you wish to take. There is time for general background and for specialization in four years of college.

Survival Strategy #11:

How to Get the Most out of Your Professors

Much too often, professors are judged prematurely as insensitive and unfair. *Not true!*

Profs have already been through college and know "the ecstasy of victory and the agony of defeat." Their attitude, surprising to many, is to be fair and give the students what they deserve. They do, on the whole, fulfill this philosophy.

By biasing themselves against profs, many students often never say more to a prof than "Here" and then the student thinks "I can't get more than a C with this prof" and therefore he works less and is worse off.

Being able to talk and communicate with a prof as a person is very valuable. Try viewing profs as people like yourselves. Offer your comments sincerely with genuine interest in him as a human being. If the prof sees you are trying to establish an honest communications network, he may be more inclined to try and see your point of view. If you show a prof you are sincerely interested, he is bound to be on your side all the way.

Many professors request information from their students, usually during the first class. They will ask for your major, career goals, previous related courses, and anything that can help them. Here is a great way to help yourself. Make yourself known. Write down accomplishments and strong points. Give the prof something different and chances are he'll take an interest in you.

When asked a question in class, never say "I don't know" or "I didn't read the chapter." This makes a poor impression and insults the prof. Take a shot at the question, to show him that at least you're interested. It is almost always better to be wrong than ignorant.

Also, when a prof is speaking and the class period is almost over, *never* shut books, click pens, or stand up—the prof wants to finish his thought without interruption.

Office Hours

Typically, profs reserve two or three hours a week for student consultation, which is voluntary and about anything the student wants to discuss. Use these time periods if you have problems or questions. Profs are usually impressed with students who take the time and have the initiative to seek out their help and guidance.

Survival Strategy #12:
Why You Should Know Your Advisors

Most departments maintain special advisors who will counsel you on problems you have. (There are usually prelaw, premed, and predental advisors to help you if needed, in addition to those in the departments.) Feel free to talk with them, and ask all the questions you have, no matter how silly they seem.

Survival Strategy #13:
How to Vary Academic Loads

The standard graduation requirement (in most colleges) of 128 credits is divided usually among eight semesters, or four years. This comes to 16 credits per semester. Three credits means three

---

hours of class per week, but in some courses you may have to put in more time for less credit. It is not always possible to take courses which total exactly 16 credits each semester: there may be a loss of credit due to transfer, major change, or other factors.

Many colleges encourage heavier credit loads to hasten graduation, so that students can get out into the working world more quickly. This has obvious advantages for some students, but it is certainly not recommended for everyone. The quality of your education is more important than the speed with which you complete your requirements. If you are interested in graduating early, it is a good idea to start off your first year with relatively light credit loads, then add to them gradually as you become more experienced at handling the work.

If you are taking too many courses and feel over-loaded, speak to your advisor *immediately* to decide if you should drop a course. Make sure to take into account the refund policy of the school on dropped courses.

Instead of dropping the course you may request an "incomplete" at some schools, usually designated by I. The deadline for such a request is usually a week before final exams begin. You will have one semester to finish the course requirements. If you don't, your I will probably turn magically into an F.

Survival Strategy #14:
How to Use Time Effectively

Time is one of the most important aspects of fitting everything in at college. Learning to utilize time properly will help you throughout life. *Time will be your master until you master it.*

Time is a funny thing. You can do more work per hour at certain times of the day when you are more aware, quicker, and more thoughtful. Planning your time includes scheduling activities and academics when your body and mind are most in tune for them.

Planning

Plan your study time. Profs regularly hand out assignments and dates for exams; if you just list them in your notes, you will often forget all about them.

My suggestion is to make up a monthly calendar on an 8½-by-11-inch sheet of paper and place all upcoming assignments, papers, tests, and activities in boxes. Now you'll be able to visualize when your time is taken up and when you're free. But if you leave your dates unorganized, you will forget something important.

Free Time

You will most likely have blocks of free time during the day between classes. I have found these times to be the best for study and homework. Your body and mind are fresh and fully rested. You become less effective as the day wears on. Besides, if you finish off the work in the morning, that leaves the evenings free!

Study Breaks

Short breaks during which you stand up and stretch, walk around, grab a bite *while still thinking about your work* are good and reenergize the mind. These periods are meant to relax you for more work and should not be abused. Wandering off, talking with friends about unrelated topics, and watching TV are no good—such distractions will draw you away from the work, which isn't the purpose of the break. Use breaks for relaxation, not for procrastination.

Tips for Commuters

Those of you who live at home and commute to college face many additional problems, most of which can be worked out easily. Make sure you have a place to park; if parking is a problem, get to campus early enough so you aren't late for class because you can't find a space.

When I commuted for two years, I found that coming to school early in the morning, perhaps an hour or two before the first class started, gave me the opportunity to take care of much on-campus work, as well as to read and write in a conducive setting like the library.

Since you don't have the convenience of an on-campus room, make sure to use the time between classes to the fullest advantage. Try to avoid traveling in the rush hour—that kind of aggravation, nobody needs.

Many colleges have commuter groups who form car pools and help each other stay abreast of campus happenings. If your school has such groups, join one.

Survival Strategy #15:
Why You Should Make Dean's List

Excellent grade achievements at most schools will result in your placement on the dean's list, a special acknowledgment of your academic efforts. Your overall cum must be up to a certain level without any grades lower than B or C (depending on the school).

Survival Strategy #16:
What Other Honors You Can Achieve

You might spend a few moments looking into the various honors in addition to dean's list that can be obtained at your college. Depending on your grade-point average, you can graduate cum laude, magna cum laude, or summa cum laude, a tremendous achievement which only a few outstanding students qualify for.

Every extra award or honor you get will add weight to your future job résumé. You'll have an edge if you can garner one or two special recognitions.

You might get elected to Phi Beta Kappa (an honor society based on outstanding academic achievement), a highly acclaimed distinction. Your department probably gives awards to distinguished students in its discipline.

Local corporations, groups, and societies also present honors in areas of research or academic achievement. Look into these possible additional honors: it may help you set another goal in addition to a high grade-point average.

Survival Strategy #17:
Why You Should Avoid Probation

You may get second chances in high school without a penalty, but you usually won't in college. Failing a course results in loss of credit; taking the course over means extra tuition. When you don't pass a course you lose money, time, and credits as well as pride.

Failure in several courses in one semester will lead to placement on the probation list. Several semesters on the pro list will probably result in your having to leave the college, permanently.

For your own sake, don't fail any courses.

College is the big time!

Survival Strategy #18:
When to Study Overseas

Every year, programs such as student exchanges, corporate programs, and direct scholarships enable students to attend universities outside the United States. Medical students may be forced to study abroad if they cannot gain acceptance at U.S. medical schools.

The advantages and disadvantages of foreign study should be considered.

Advantages

1. There is the opportunity to live in a different country, to be a part of their customs and life-style.

2. It is a once-in-a-lifetime chance to study overseas; it is only available to selected students.

3. Overseas study permits special research utilizing resources not available in the U.S.

4. Language majors can master their chosen language in its natural setting.

Disadvantages

1. You may have to learn a second language and do all your studies in that language. This is more difficult than it sounds.

2. You will have to live away from home, with probably less comforts and luxuries than you'll find here.

3. You'll be living in a foreign country with customs and social norms different from what you are used to.

Investigate overseas studying thoroughly before you decide. You'll have to apply for a leave of absence, and may have to reapply to get back into an American college. Most American colleges are on two semesters per year, but foreign schools may have three (called trimesters). You will have to straighten out your credits between two unmatched arrangements, and you may not get the credits, when you return, that you feel you have earned.

Talking to your major advisor is important: your school may be affiliated with a foreign school and this will clear up some of the above-mentioned obstacles.

Studying overseas takes a lot of careful planning, thinking, and making sure it's what you want.

Survival Strategy #19:

When to Consider Transferring or Exchange Programs

The competition to gain admission to certain colleges is tough; therefore, many students get to the college of their choice by a back-door method. After studying for two years at a lesser-known or a community college, they apply for transfer to a more prestigious college. If accepted, they eventually receive their diploma from the better school.

Transferring is common as a means of upgrading

education, moving closer to or farther away from home, or easing financial burdens.

Transfer procedures are fairly straightforward, but the application of credits earned in the first school toward the degree requirements of the second school can become complex and frustrating.

If you are thinking about transferring, it is wise to find out which courses will be accepted at the second school, and which will be rejected. It doesn't make sense to take two years of courses at a community college and then have ten credits not approved when you make your move. Every course you have to repeat means a longer stay in college and more money spent.

Transferring can put you up against stiff competition; it may not be worth the effort if you are aware of this. Many transfers, unfortunately, are "blind" . . . the student has no idea whether or not he'll like the school he transfers to.

There is a very limited exchange program, available at scattered universities throughout the country, which overcomes this problem by giving the student two exposures of college. Let's say you're now enrolled at Blue College, and are interested in transferring to Red University. If the schools have this program, you can remain enrolled at Blue and study for a year at Red, with credits to be applied at Blue or Red. At the end of the year you can stay at Blue and receive full credits, or apply for transfer to Red and also receive full credits. Check the admissions office of your school to see if such a program is available.

Survival Strategy #20:

How to Use Your College's Resources

What you learn in college is part of success after college. Equally important are the people you meet and talk with, and the sources of information you discover.

College department chairpeople receive "tons" of literature every day from scores of organizations and colleges. These books, pamphlets, announcements, and flyers are usually available to the student, enabling you to discover many sources where people are eager to help you as a young college student. There are many little-known magazines, groups, and associations which can be very valuable in your future job placement.

Some examples of the information available to you as a student are:

- a brochure from a national biology or chemical society describing current trends, job openings, and the predicted future course of the industry

- a newsletter from a regional federal agency which informs the student of little-known employment opportunities

- a trade magazine from the marketing profession especially written for students designed to provide them with an insight into the various segments of sales, advertising, promotion, and marketing

- a journalism internship program available at participating newspapers, magazines, and radio and TV stations

- a current listing of unadvertised positions open in a specific field

The variety of information available is amazing.

Many jobs are available to students that go beyond library, cafeteria, and desk work. They are at specific departments and call for lab assistants, paper graders, etc. It is an excellent way to become involved in your special interest field, and there are many benefits you can receive, including postgraduate job recommendations and inside information.

Become familiar with the career placement office on campus. This is a clearinghouse for job-related information coming into the college, including fulltime, part-time, and summer jobs. Alumni may have job offers or may donate time to counsel students in their field. Consult them when you're ready. The current announcements of openings, usually on a bulletin board, should be consulted regularly. Get to know the placement director; a personal relationship may lead to him calling you before someone else.

Your freshman advisor is also a valuable source of information and help; he is qualified to help you with any problem—academic, personal adjustment, roommate quarrels, homesick feelings. Know who your advisor is, as well as the dean of men or women.

Survival Strategy #21:
Why You Should Join Clubs

One of the best ways to develop your area of interest, make friends while meeting people with common interests and goals, and learn to function in an organization is to join clubs and professional fraternities.

Every campus has an endless number of these groups, from the campus newspaper to a highly technical club in one of the sciences. You'll gain the most practical experiences possible from joining one or more of these clubs. Most clubs get together on career planning and work on group projects. You may help create a magazine, write it, edit it, sell advertising space in it, print it, and sell it on campus. Just from this experience you get a taste of many careers: writer, editor, salesperson, business manager, artist, printer, advertising person, general manager.

A semester project of a psychology club may involve library research and lab experimentation to test out hypotheses. A field survey may be taken and the results tabulated on the university's computer. The results may even be published in one of the psychology profession's many journals! This is an opportunity for you to gain practical experience and communicate with people already working in the field.

This kind of participation in real projects can be as valuable as the material learned in class and read in texts. If a club or group is available that you're interested in, join it!

Survival Strategy #22:
What Are the Living Alternatives?

Dormitories

This is the most popular choice of where to live at college, because a dorm is an easy place to live and the best place to find other young people just starting out in college. Many colleges have freshman dorms.

After a year or two in a dormitory, you'll be better able to decide whether it suits your style.

Dorm life is characterized by friendly camaraderie, with perhaps a noisier atmosphere than is always desirable. Most students do not do all that much studying in the dorm but rather in the library or other quiet places. Dorms usually have faculty and/or student resident advisors to handle special problems that may arise.

There is one important point to be made about roommate(s). You will be given a roommate without knowing him/her, and getting along with your roomie is very important; you don't need any extra problems with an inconsiderate roommate. If problems such as entertaining too late, making noise while studying, or not keeping the room as clean as is reasonable crop up, you must talk with your roommate, be firm, and clear up the problems before they become habits. If you are the one guilty of inconsiderate behavior, correct it before your roommate has to speak to you.

Many colleges send out questionnaires to entering students to help match you up with an appropriate roommate. Write down the way you are, not the way you want someone else to be; it is your personal interests that they want to see. Don't room with someone from your hometown. College is a place to make friends and meet people from all over the country, not to keep your hometown way of thinking.

A good way to avoid conflict with a roommate is to set up ground rules from the first day. Talk with your roommate and merge your common goals into a living arrangement that will suit you both.

Fraternities and Sororities

The campus fraternities and sororities, for men and women respectively, are socially oriented organizations, although they are academically involved to some degree.

A fraternity offers the freshman a place to hang his or her hat, a group living arrangement where cooking and other chores can be shared, and an opportunity to schedule group social events and parties more than is possible in dorm life.

Some frats also maintain files of term papers (for reference only!), texts, notes, and other helpful academic information. These groups provide a brotherly or sisterly common bond which may be just the thing for you.

In the opening weeks of the semester the fraternities and sororities make their sales pitches, attempting to get new members. Visit their open houses and talk with the men or women there. In general, each frat house has a special type of person who lives there. You'll probably have to weed out a few fraternities to find the kind of house you'll be happy in.

Pledge week comes next: you indicate your desire

to join a specific frat, and upon acceptance, you're initiated, usually with the typical collegiate hazing everyone knows about, which may include scrubbing the floor with a toothbrush or polishing a senior's car.

Frats and sororities can be good places to make friendships and have a good time, but they do tend—with some exceptions—to be a little more on the social than the academic side of college. Make sure that your work doesn't suffer.

Private Quarters

Once you've made friends at college, opportunities will arise for you to live in apartments or houses, usually off campus, with one to five schoolmates of your choice. In such a joint effort, all bills, duties, and work toward the upkeep of a house or apartment are shared.

Obviously, it is most important to choose people to live with who are compatible with you. Check out your prospective co-renters to see if they meet these requirements:

- they are committed to achieving good grades (i.e., not the person who takes gut courses and has time to play)

- their personalities and temperaments fit in with yours

- they can afford the bills and will pay their share on time

- they will consistently take care of their share of household chores

One point about the financial and bill-paying aspect of living in a group: usually the phone and other bills are under one person's name, who is responsible for all the others. If you are that person, get an advance deposit from everyone, keeping enough money in the kitty to pay all bills on time. There have been many problems with roommates who run up enormous long-distance phone bills and don't pay them. Don't let it happen to you!

Survival Strategy #23:
How to Keep Your Body (and Mind) Healthy

Our country is becoming increasingly sports-minded. This is great, since your body, like your mind, needs constant stimulation, and your physical well-being affects your mental efficiency.

Most colleges offer athletic programs on the intercollegiate varsity level, on the intracollege club level, and on an individual free-time basis. Whatever your sport, there will always be someone to play tennis with or choose up in a basketball game, pickup style.

There are many sports to choose from, and organized competition makes it more interesting. Swimming is a good all-around sport for keeping in shape; it uses many of the muscles in your body. Running is very popular these days, as are racquetball and tennis.

You should aim to play ball or participate in athletics at least two or three times a week. Once a week is not as good as three times a week, even if the total time spent working out is the same. Three short workouts are better than one long one. The object here is to exercise frequently and steadily—not sporadically.

If you study a lot, and therefore sit a lot, exercise is even more important. Your circulation must be steady and free-flowing, and continuous sitting without exercising certainly won't achieve that.

Choose the sport from the list below which fits your preferences.

OUTDOOR

Team:
baseball
football
soccer
tennis
softball
rugby
ice hockey
field hockey

Individual:
running
track and field
golf

INDOOR

Team:
basketball
gymnastics
volleyball

Individual:
swimming
fencing
squash
tennis
racquetball
handball
paddleball
dance
weight-lifting
wrestling
water polo

Work up to a goal slowly. If you're weight-lifting, don't start out trying to show off as a strong man. If you're a long-distance runner, don't expect to cover 15 miles the first day out. Your body resists sudden large changes, but responds well to gradual build-ups to your goals.

Another aspect of keeping healthy is what you eat. The typical collegiate diet seems to be 95 percent junk food, but you don't have to accept that. Living on your own means you get to choose what you eat. Don't try to keep alive on pizza, hot dogs, and fries. Be sure to eat a balanced diet, including plenty of fruits, vegetables, and protein.

If the food in the dining halls is not up to your standards, consider supplementing it with healthy snacks, like nuts, cheese, and fruit. Some colleges rent small fridges that can be shared by roommates at reasonable cost. This means you can shop at the local supermarket or college store. Parents can usually be encouraged to send CARE packages during the semester as well.

3
THE
READING

3

Too many students leave the reading required for courses until a few days before an exam is scheduled or a paper is due, rather than reading steadily throughout the term, which is much more effective in terms of retention and understanding.

Survival Strategy #24:

How to Time Your Reading

You must plan your required reading on a weekly basis, according to a specific schedule—usually, the one outlined on your syllabus. If no schedule is given you, you should break up the readings into equal sections yourself. (see p. 51.) Leaving the reading for the last minute is bad:

1. Before taking an exam or writing a paper (assuming this is what the readings are aimed at), you have to prepare yourself under pressure of time. If you have already completed the reading assignment, your studying, reviewing the reading, or writing is done under less pressure. Less time pressure means better test results or a better term paper. Having to read, review, and cram one or two nights before an exam is too much pressure. When you have a constant feeling of "deadline," you cannot fully comprehend what you're reading.

2. A prerequisite to success in any exam is understanding the course material. As has been proved by psychologists, spaced practice (learning with rest periods—in this case, spreading the reading over the whole semester) is better than massed practice (cramming). Steady, bit-by-bit reading gives better absorption of the material.

3. In many courses, such as philosophy and sociology, the work read must be thought over, and your own views incorporated into what has been read. If you read the required pages at a leisurely rate, you'll be able to mull over what you've read and form your own conclusions and ideas. Also, questions and problems you raise while reading can be examined more closely or noted for research later. This can't be done effectively the night before an exam.

4. There is a maximum threshold connecting quantity of reading material and absorption of its content. Beyond the saturation level, you become ineffective in understanding additional material. The pages read after you reach this limit are useless for the exam. Never overload yourself with more pages than you can adequately absorb.

5. Leisurely reading brings a more relaxed viewpoint, which leads to better and easier understanding; it also enables you to correlate lecture material with the information read in the text.

Survival Strategy #25:
What Is the Best Setting?

Traditional modes of reading while watching "Star Trek" or listening to Grand Funk Railroad produce "destructive interference," resulting in a vague perception of the material read.

It takes much longer to complete a reading assignment while the boob tube is on. The reading is not fully digested and the show or music is not fully enjoyed, because your energy is divided between the two.

Everybody worries about where to study. Some students can study in a dorm, but others need the library, and others prefer the cafeteria. I've found the best place to be one where you'll find:

- other people studying too, so you're surrounded by people doing what you're doing

- quiet, because concentration is so very important

- comfortable chairs and good lighting

Try to study in the same place every day. Good habits work wonders!

Survival Strategy #26:
How to Underline

Underlining important sentences is a very useful technique. Highlighting the material with yellow magic markers, bright flair pens, or ordinary pens or pencils aids you in several ways:

1. It teaches you to pick out the important facts or underlying theme(s) of the passage(s) read, and to set key sentences aside for future reference.

2. While underlining, you have a look at the important material a second time; the repetition leads to a better understanding and remembering.

3. In long passages or books, material that is not underlined usually doesn't have to be studied for an exam. Underlining will save you a lot of rereading time.

Be careful and thorough, making sure to underline all the important material. What is important is determined by the nature of the work, the degree to which the material will be covered on the test, and the reputation of the prof when it comes to asking trivial questions.

But don't go to extremes and underline everything. Don't underline words that are only there to make the sentence read easier. Examples follow.

TOO MUCH UNDERLINING

One of the most elementary reactions is the <u>ionic combination in a water solution of sodium (Na) and chlorine (Cl) to get NaCl, which is commonly called table salt.</u>

<u>This paper is concerned with the socialization of new managers by the companies they join. The focus will be on</u> the effect of the <u>company's initial expectations of the young</u> managers <u>upon their</u> subsequent <u>performance</u> and success.

<u>Net profit is easily defined</u> as the <u>amount of money left over</u> for the <u>owner's personal use after all expenses and</u> taxes have been paid.

The <u>universe or population is the total group from which the sample is selected; the frequency distribution of a universe</u> may be <u>approximated by the random sample, a miniature replica of the universe.</u>

GOOD UNDERLINING

One of the most elementary reactions is the <u>ionic combination</u> in a <u>water solution</u> of <u>sodium (Na)</u> and <u>chlorine (Cl)</u> to get <u>NaCl,</u> which is commonly called <u>table salt.</u>

This paper is concerned with the <u>socialization of new managers</u> by the companies they join. The <u>focus</u> will be on the <u>effect</u> of the company's initial expectations of the <u>young</u> managers <u>upon their</u> subsequent <u>performance</u> and success.

<u>Net profit</u> is easily defined as the <u>amount</u> of money <u>left over</u> for the owner's <u>personal use</u> after all <u>expenses and</u> taxes have been paid.

The <u>universe or population</u> is the <u>total group from which</u> the <u>sample</u> is <u>selected;</u> the <u>frequency distribution</u> of a universe may be <u>approximated</u> by the <u>random sample,</u> a <u>miniature replica</u> of the universe.

Many students never seem to *use* their textbooks. It looks as if they leave their texts spotless in order to sell them at the end of the semester.

Use your text! Underline with bright colors! Make notes to yourself at strategic points! Write in your own definitions! Cross out big words and put in words you understand! Scribble in the margins!

Survival Strategy #27:
Taking Notes on Your Reading

Note taking while reading a textbook chapter isn't very common among students, but I have found it saves a great deal of time, especially the night before an exam. By first underlining and then summarizing all the passages I have underlined, I end up with a concise review of the material read, on a couple of sheets of paper. There are two advantages to using this method.

1. Learning of the material is hastened by writing it down. Now it has been read, underlined, and noted, making three memory exposures.

2. Condensing 500 or more pages into 10 to 20 pages eliminates hours of turning pages and searching for underlined sections.

In the example given a few pages back on the table salt chemical reaction, the highlighted sentence can be noted in many ways, e.g.:

$$\text{sodium} + \text{chlorine} \xrightarrow[\text{water soln.}]{\text{ionic comb.}} \text{NaCl (table salt)}$$

This clear statement (written with your own customary abbreviations) will be easily understood when you are reviewing for an exam.

Survival Strategy #28:

What Is the Best Attitude Toward Reading?

Approach your readings with an open and questioning attitude. Read slowly and carefully, evaluating facts and carefully considering interpretations of those facts. A word of caution: Do not automatically accept everything you read. Remember that books are written by people, who, like yourself, have definite points of view. In addition to mastering the material presented in your readings, learn to sharpen your own powers of observation.

Be sure not to rush yourself as you read. Read at a steady pace, but don't turn the page until you feel you understand what you just read. By spending a little more time on your readings, you'll be better prepared for class, and better able to participate in discussion. And you'll save yourself a lot of time, effort and panic when exams roll around.

Survival Strategy #29:

How to Organize Your Reading

In one course, we were assigned 242 pages (20 chapters) of reading, on which we would be tested in six weeks.

Step 1: I made a schedule, since none was provided: 242 pages divided by 5 weeks (allow for unexpected circumstances) = about 50 pages per week. I broke this up into two sittings of 20 and 30 pages each.

Step 2: In the absolute quiet of my room, while as relaxed as possible, I read the material, underlining what was important. After reading and highlighting, I compiled notes.

Total elapsed time (20 pages): about 45 minutes. After five weeks of nonpressured reading, I had a concise set of notes which served as an excellent study guide for the exam. Review was easy, and I remembered most of the material without even having tried to memorize it.

Survival Strategy #30:

How to Read Faster

The average student is not aware of how fast he can read. Two simple suggestions will increase your reading speed and comprehension.

1. Move your index finger along the line you are reading; go line after line without hesitating between. If you find you're reading ahead of your finger, move it faster and faster until you feel yourself gliding through the material.

2. Never read without using your finger as a movement guide, or you'll find yourself reading slower and daydreaming, and your understanding will decrease.

Sometimes you can speed-read to survey a course. If you have a choice between three appealing courses any of which will meet your requirements, you can skim through borrowed copies of the texts in one night and get a quick feeling about each course's material. However, speed-reading should not be used to race through a text in time for "Monday Night Football"!

4
NOTE
TAKING

4

Probably the most important written material you will collect is your notes on lectures. (For notes on reading, see p. 49.)

In all but a few courses, the day-in, day-out pages of notes will be your major source of information to review for an exam. Good notes are highly important to academic success. What a professor chooses to lecture about is most likely to appear on the exam. The importance of neat, sophisticated notes may be illustrated as follows:

1. Notes are your personal way of expressing, sometimes in a form discernible only by you, your reactions to a lecture.

2. Taking notes is the prime means of obtaining information and keeping it handy for studying for exams.

3. Note taking is a learning process. While you write the notes, you are automatically memorizing some of what you're writing.

Most students don't know how to take notes well. Here is my personal method: it will give you notes that are great for review before an examination.

Survival Strategy #31:

How to Organize Your Note Taking

Your goal should be a clean set of complete notes that will be a useful study tool later on. To do that, I copy over my notes after class—a little more work—but well worth it in the long run.

You will probably respond, "This just isn't possible . . . I'll never have time to copy my notes." That's a typical reaction, but one you might regret later. By copying your notes over, you will be reinforcing your knowledge and understanding of what just went on in class. By translating your notes into *your own words*—not the professor's—you will really save time when it's test-time, because you will really *know* that material. Your studying will involve review, not learning. And you'll have time to concentrate on those tricky areas that may have been giving you trouble.

You don't have to take neat notes in class if you are going to copy them. They just have to be neat enough for you to read them later. Try to get as much down during the lecture as possible, using shorthand, symbols, abbreviations, slang, etc., to make it easier.

One symbol which I found can take the place of many words is the arrow, which can be used to connect thoughts and statements:

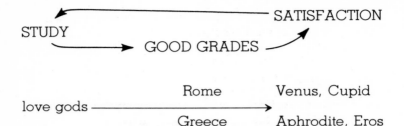

In the first example the arrows replace a wordy "Study results in good grades, which lead to satisfaction, which fosters further study, good grades, etc." The arrows imply circularity and regularity.

In the second example, the arrow takes the place of "The love gods of ancient Rome and Greece were Venus and Cupid, and Aphrodite and Eros, respectively."

Everyone uses arrows in the sciences, especially in chemical reactions, but you can use them for any subject.

Another symbol that saves time is the Greek letter delta, $\triangle$, which means "change" (in mathematics). In today's rapidly changing society, it is a word that pops up in every course. And the words "changed," "changing," and "changeable" can be shortened to $\triangle$ d, $\triangle$ ing, and $\triangle$ able.

Several other symbols and abbreviations which make note taking easier and more effective follow.

+	plus, positive
−	minus, negative
↑	increase, higher
↓	decrease, lower
=	equal
=ly	equally

>	greater than
<	less than
≠	not equal
e.g.	for example
wrt	with respect to
w/	with
w/i	within
w/o	without
wh/	which
4	for
∴	therefore
info	information
approx	approximate(ly)
re	reference, referring to
etc	and so forth, etcetera
bec	because
avg	average
∞	infinity, infinite

These symbols are not my own creation. They are commonly used in all fields. The more you can use them in each course, the better your note taking will become.

In class, write notes to yourself in the margins: reminders of assignments, questions, and prof's suggestions. Don't leave it all to your memory, or you'll forget those useful little hints the profs give: "Don't be surprised if you see some questions from this chapter on the final exam."

After class, in a quiet place, set aside 20 minutes for each subject to copy your notes. Same-day copying is recommended, since the material will be fresh in your mind.

As you copy your notes, you may have in front of you a sloppy mess of material which can now be copied over in a neat format, with the symbols and abbreviations expanded if desired. Leave out any material you now see is irrelevant. Leave wide margins for extra (future) material. You can under-line the sections the prof says are important. This helps you predict what will appear in future examinations.

The end product is a set of precise, excellent notes which present the lecture even more clearly than the prof did.

At the end of the notes for each lecture, summarize in one paragraph the major points covered. You may want to use a different color of ink. Use your own words: you'll understand them better when you review in several weeks.

Survival Strategy #32:
How to Set Up Your Notes

The form of your notes depends on what they're ued for. Class notes, to be used later in studying for an exam, should be in a three-ring binder. You can take notes in class on regular lined paper, but copy them on paper which fits the binder. Professors sometimes have a habit of skipping around; with a loose-leaf binder you can always insert additional material in the right place.

If your notes will be used to write a paper, it is best to use 5x7 lined cards. You can use a simple and effective method to organize your cards, bibliography, and footnotes all at once.

First, list all your sources, giving the book or magazine article's title, author, publisher, date, and city. (Now most of your bibliography is done.) Assign a letter of the alphabet to each source. This will be your master reference card.

On a second card, make a rough outline of the topics you wish to cover. They don't have to be in order, but use one line for each topic you think you will need notes on.

Now you are ready to begin the actual note taking. When you find something you would like to jot down, first put the source letter in the upper left-hand corner of your notecard. Then, on the first line below that, write down the topic of the notes to follow on that card. The notes themselves follow. They may consist of facts, exact quotes (indicate with quote marks), or an interpretation in your own words of what you have read. Keep the notes brief, but easy to understand. Be sure to list the page number from your source for each note so that you can properly footnote your paper later on without having to go back to the original source.

Here are two samples of what your note cards might look like:

A
  Automobiles
    (foreign makes)
 	
  p. 7: Porsche/Audi/
    Volkswagen
	D
	Automobiles
	    (American makes)
	
	p. 33: Chrysler/Ford
	p. 34: Chevrolet

5
WRITING PAPERS

5

Papers play an important role in almost every course. They may even be the sole criterion in determining your grade. My technique, which I apply to all papers, has been very successful over the years.

Survival Strategy #33:
How to Organize Your Paper Writing

There are four major steps in writing a good paper.

Research

Research determines the success of the paper—assuming you can write it properly. A well-researched paper is simpler and easier to write. Research consists of two main steps.

1. *Definition of the Topic.* The topic is usually assigned by the prof, or he may list the general areas that are acceptable. You can't just generalize—you must choose something specific.

Selecting a topic is difficult (when the selection is left to you). Here are some ways to check if you have chosen a good topic.

A. Does the topic meet any requirements set forth by the professor? Is it in the assigned subject area?

B. Does the topic stick to the main issue, or does it cover a tangent or unimportant offshoot?

C. Will you be able to find enough material?

D. Will you be able to answer the essential questions in the space allotted?

E. Is the topic informative, interesting, and/or creative?

F. Has the topic been mentioned or implied by the prof in class?

If you can answer yes to all six questions, you have chosen a good topic.

2. *Obtaining Information.* Efficient collection of information entails becoming as knowledgeable as possible on the topic, getting as much information as you can. It is better to overlearn than learn "just enough":

A. You should have many viewpoints of

the same material so you can present a realistic picture.

B. Your ability to offer different explanations shows the prof *you* are proficient on the subject, and that you have not just copied someone's work.

C. If you have plenty of material, you can select only the important facts, using concise examples and material which suits your needs best.

Gathering ample material shows the prof you have researched thoroughly. Most profs hate "bulling"—you are better off giving facts than spouting meaningless generalizations.

Try to collate information from books, magazine articles, and other sources on note cards so that cross-checking between many volumes is avoided and time is saved. (See chapter four.)

The library is the obvious source of data for your research. Most college libraries are well organized, and the materials available are abundant and varied. Besides textbooks and hardcover books on specific topics, there are periodicals, records, tapes, microfilm, and other sources.

Librarians are among the most helpful people you'll ever meet. Don't try to figure out where to get information by yourself. Save time and ask the librarian: you'll be steered in the right direction by a person who knows what's in print. Your prof or department head probably knows some valuable sources. Ask him.

Actual Writing

The writing is where you must take your time. You must choose your words carefully and say *exactly what you mean.* If you read over your reference notes several times before starting to write, you will become aware of where the important facts are noted, and you'll be able to pull them out when needed.

Besides extracting the material from carefully researched notes, you must write paragraphs that are coherent and smooth; transitions between them should flow evenly. If you give examples or quotes be sure to cite your sources.

Research should be finished one or two days before writing begins. The time you will spend writing, of course, depends on the length of the paper.

LENGTH OF PAPER (pages)	WRITING TIME (weeks)
1-5	½
6-10	1½
11-15	3
16-30	6
31-	8

These are double-spaced, typewritten pages. Write a very short paper in one sitting if possible.

NEVER TYPE A PAPER ON
THE SAME DAY IT WAS WRITTEN

Review and Revision

After the first draft of the paper has been written, leave it alone for a day (or longer) and then come back to it. Read it coldly. Make corrections and don't hesitate to rewrite any section (no matter how long) that doesn't say *exactly* what you want it to. Read the paper aloud so you can hear your writing and judge it word by word. This often helps in catching grammatical errors.

The reasons for waiting a day before revising a paper are:

1. You will be so relieved to have a finished paper that chances are you won't be able to criticize it objectively immediately afterward. After waiting, you'll be able to read the paper more coldly and impersonally and will be able to evaluate it better.

2. While waiting, thoughts not included in the first draft may pop up; also, unimportant material will more easily be eliminated.

3. Information is reprocessed subconsciously; you may find a better way to express a given thought.

Typing

All papers should be typed and double-spaced unless you are told otherwise. The importance of correct spelling, punctuation, and grammar, and of proofreading for typing errors, cannot be overemphasized.

Use ample margins, 2 inches at the top and bottom and 1½ inches at the sides. Professors know, however, when you increase the margins further to make your paper longer.

Survival Strategy #34:
How to Set Up Footnotes Properly

Consult your professor to find out if there is a school-wide policy for footnotes or bibliography. Or consult a reference book such as the ones listed in Survival Strategy #4.

Footnotes are used when you quote another work in your paper, to credit the author who wrote the particular sentence or passage. Omitting footnotes is a form of plagiarism, and profs condemn that. Usually, each quotation is set off in quotation marks ("To be or not to be") and is identified by a raised number at the end of the quote: "Art is long, and Time is fleeting."[5]

At the foot of the page on which the quote is typed, use this format to give credit for the work:

[1]Irv Brechner, The College Survival Kit (New York: Bantam Books, 1979), p. 18.

[2]Barbara W. Tuchman, "If Asia Were Clay in the Hands of the West," Atlantic, September 1970, p. 72.

[3]Paul Tillich, "Being and Love," in Moral Principles of Action, ed. Ruth N. Anshen (New York: Harper & Row, 1952), p. 663.

Survival Strategy #35:

How to Set Up
Bibliographies Correctly

The bibliography lists all the sources you have used in writing your paper. The professor will supplement his opinion of your paper by considering the quantity and quality of your bibliographic references.

The bibliography is one way to help a prof evaluate your paper, check on the validity of your staements, and see how thorough you have been. It gives the paper credibility and the sources to back up statements.

Don't beef up the bibliography with books you didn't use—profs know what the good references are and will quickly recognize a padded bibliography.

List the sources by author according to the following format:

Brechner, Irv. The College Survival Kit. New York: Bantam Books, 1979.
Tillich, Paul. "Being and Love." In Moral Principles of Action, pp. 661–72. Edited by Ruth N. Anshen. New York: Harper & Row, 1952.
Tuchman; Barbara W. "If Asia Were Clay in the Hands of the West." Atlantic, September 1970, pp. 68–84.

As with footnotes, be complete, and follow the rules.

Survival Strategy #36:
Why Good Titles Are Necessary

Professors read many papers on the same or similar topics. They get tired of seeing the same old run-of-the-mill titles, and welcome papers with creative titles which stand out. A good title gets you off on the right foot.

Instead of the poor title "How Carbon and Oxygen React," try the good title "Some Interesting Reactions Between Oxygen and Carbon."

Instead of "Semester Review of Philosophy 101," try "A Semester of Introspection and Analysis: Philosophy 101."

Instead of "Catch-22 Book Review," try "What the Catch Is in Catch-22."

Survival Strategy #37:
How Papers Are Graded

Papers are graded according to what the prof expects and what the class as a whole produces. After reading several papers without grading them, the prof sees the general pattern of writing and thought. He compares your individual paper with the trend and with his ideas of what you should have written.

You may feel the prof has graded you unfairly. Don't waste time . . . make an appointment to see the professor in his office and present your arguments. Most profs are reasonable and will give you the benefit of any doubt. But be prepared to back up your claims with a solid argument. That is the only way you'll move a professor to change his mind.

6
EXAMINA-
TIONS

6

Exams are the most important part of college life today. Everything you do, whether going to class or participating in outside activities, revolves around the test schedule you're given.

Called by a variety of names—tests, quizzes, exams—they have one thing in common: they tend to be a lot harder than most students expect. Don't underestimate their scope and difficulty. The cause of harder exams (compared to high-school tests) is the relative sophistication of the work and the shorter college schedule.

Survival Strategy #38:

Be Prepared

Exams usually cover a lot of material—whole textbooks, additional outside readings, and countless pages of notes—so a wealth of information must be memorized. Be prepared by studying *everything* that could possibly be asked, not just selectively memorizing what you think the prof will ask. If you study it all, you'll never study the wrong material; and you won't be caught outwitting yourself.

Survival Strategy #39:
College vs. High-School Exams

Unlike high-school tests, which are mostly about names, dates, and places, college exams usually test your understanding of the material rather than your ability to memorize facts. They test your ability to apply your knowledge of a subject to a problem, situation, or case.

Survival Strategy #40:
Forget About Curves and Scales

Many students rationalize about studying, saying: "Well, since the class I'm in usually does poorly, I can study less and count on the scale to bring up my grade." This is counted on so often, but it just doesn't work. By studying less and less, you get into a rut, and soon you'll find that the scale merely keeps you from getting an F. This may work once or twice, but in the long run (four years) your terrible study habits will hurt your grades in every course you take.

Profs don't like to grade on a scale. By scaling down they are hurting the students who study and helping the loafers.

Survival Strategy #41:
Why You Shouldn't Cut Tests

There are few good excuses for missing a test. Profs hate to compose makeup tests, and to ward off cutters most profs give makeups that are much harder than the original. Also, the prof has no way of knowing if the makeup test is fair. If he grades 20 or 30 original tests, he may conclude that one or more of his questions are unfair and make allowances. He won't do this for one student on a makeup.

Survival Strategy #42:
Different Types of Exams

There are two kinds of exams—objective and subjective. You'll be exposed to both—more often, to a combination of the two.

Objective Tests

Objective exams call for brief answers. You may be asked to fill in a blank, to match items in one column with those in another, or to respond to multiple-choice, short-answer, or true/false questions. It is common, especially in psychology, to find tests composed solely of multiple-choice questions (often called multiple-guess); in other courses you may find all true/false or definition exams.

It is a common mistake to think that objective tests are easy because all the possible answers are given. This is not true. The trend is toward "think" questions which present you with three to five almost equally probable answers. You have to choose the best one for full credit.

Objective exams are tougher than essay exams because an answer is either right or wrong; there are no in-betweens, no room for personal opinion. The answers cannot be hastily chosen. You must carefully eliminate choices until you are left with the one you think best answers the question. Many such questions have answers which differ by only one word.

Thinking out the question is essential, and you will need a complete knowledge of theory as well as facts.

Here is an example:

The most likely reason why a magazine like *The Saturday Evening Post* went out of business is because:

    (1) the price of the magazine was too high
    (2) it couldn't sell enough advertising
    (3) the magazine was too general
    (4) people got tired of it
    (5) the printing quality was not that good

The correct answer is (2). One assumption made is that the magazine got its revenue from advertising, so that is the best reason why it went out of business. Answers (3) and (4) are supporting reasons why they couldn't sell advertising. Answer (5) should be disregarded because the printing was fine and (1) is not important because the price was no higher than other magazines.

A typical objective exam usually consists of about 50 questions (the range is from 25 to 125). In shorter tests the questions are very thought-provoking; the longer exams require more straightforward information.

When asking true/false questions, profs like to tempt you with statements which are half true and half false. For a question to be answered "True," *all* of it must be true *all* the time.

It is common while taking an exam to have the answer on the tip of your tongue. If you blank out (forget) something you know, put your head on your desk for a few minutes. Your posture will change, your brain position will be altered, and you'll become relaxed. This sometimes will help you remember the information.

Objective Problem Tests

These tests are common in science, math, and business courses. Often there are 3 to 15 problems of varying degrees of difficulty.

The way to study for these exams is to do sample problems over and over, until you're proficient. You have to know the subject, too, to know which formula to use or what values to plug in.

Always look at the problem carefully before you start writing. One tricky thing profs like to do (actually a giveaway) is give a long, seemingly very complex problem whose answer turns out to be very simple, maybe 0 or 1:

$$x = \left(\frac{6352 - 1575 \ \sqrt{25} + 3.67}{2575 - 23\pi}\right)\left(\frac{5 - \sqrt{25}}{245}\right)\left(\frac{616.6 \times 10^8}{24}\right)$$

The middle multiplier in this problem is equal to zero, so $x = 0$!

Such problems look so hard that many students skip them. Yet the example just given takes ten seconds to solve in your head.

Another common trick, used by chemistry profs, is to put two chemicals on the left-hand side of an equation and ask you to show the result of their reaction on the right-hand side. But they are chemicals that do not react with each other, so the answer is a blank or "No reaction." Don't assume, like many students do, that a reaction (or any outcome) must take place simply because of the format of the question.

These examples show how profs test you. They aren't asking anything unfair if you've studied. They'll continue to throw in these questions to better help them evaluate you.

Many science exams include nonproblem questions that ask for diagrams, drawings, reactions, explanations of physical phenomena, etc. Make your drawings crisp, clean, and accurate.

Follow this method consistently when taking any type of objective exam: first answer the questions and/or problems you are sure of, and come back to the more difficult ones later on; this builds confidence.

Timing in test taking is important. Don't spend a lot of time on one question unless it's worth a big hunk of the exam; check your watch every 10 to 20 minutes during a 50-minute exam so you know where you stand.

Always leave 5 minutes before the end to check your answers, making sure there are no careless errors. Many times a plus or minus sign will cost you several points. Check that you used exactly the values given in the question, with no accidental changes.

Subjective Tests

Subjective tests are also called essay exams, since they require essays of various lengths and difficulty. Your answers will show the prof (1) whether or not you have learned and understand the material and (2) if you can express yourself to say what you mean.

A prof grades essay tests by asking himself these questions:

1. Does the student know the correct answer and come right out and say it clearly and concisely?

2. Or does he have a vague idea and try to make up for what he doesn't know by bulling?

There are five basic steps you should follow for every question in a subjective exam:

1. READ all the questions before you answer any. Work on the easiest ones first.

2. UNDERLINE important facts and key words.

3. THINK for at least one minute about your answer—don't write the first thought that pops into your mind.

4. WRITE, taking your time and being accurate.

5. At the end, leave time to PROOFREAD for any kind of error.

It is better to overlearn than to risk underlearning. If you can relate many facts to one topic, it shows the prof you have studied well. Three cautions:

1. Answer the question. Don't stray off on a tangent with extraneous information.

2. Use extra material only after the question has been answered; not instead of answering it.

3. Don't include so much extra material that you drown out the basic answr.

Profs mention three types of errors that are the most common stumbling blocks:

1. Some students give only generalizations without valid support and examples.

2. Others give a million facts but no reasons; they forget to state the whys and the hows.

3. Still others write five almost unrelated paragraphs. Don't do this: organize your work!

There is one big *don't* about essay tests: Unless the instructions specifically call for short answers, it is never wise to write a skimpy answer, one that gives the impression that you are unknowledgeable. Avoid an undetailed outline. Explain everything!

Survival Strategy #43:

Midterms and Final Exams

Increasingly, course testing is being confined to two exams: the midterm and the final. Together they account for most of the final grade: the final alone may count for 50% to 70% of the grade.

Many students like having only two tests to study for. But actually you're lucky if you have three or four exams, since you won't be overly penalized if you have an off day.

Midterms

Midterm exams are given around Halloween and before Easter recess. Your midterms will usually fall within a two-week period; you will be under a lot of pressure.

A natural consequence of this flurry of exams is the "all-nighter," when a student stays up all night to study, only to fall asleep during or even miss the next day's exam. Don't stay up all night studying . . . it isn't worth it.

Instead of the all-nighter, prepare for the exam for several days in advance. By continually going over the material, it can be learned without loss of sleep and sanity.

When the midterm is the only test besides the final, if you don't do well on it, you'll have plenty of pressure on the final, so don't take the midterm lightly.

Finals

Finals are usually given in a two-hour time slot, but average completion time is only 1¼ to 1½ hours if you know the subject. The number of questions on an objective final ranges from 50 to 300: and on essay and problem finals, from 5 to 25.

Finals are *the* exams: they either make or break you. The most common method of study is to give up all outside activities, pull many all-nighters, and concentrate solely on studying in the two-week exam period.

Just not good. I'll show you a better way.

Survival Strategy #44:

The New Method of Studying for Finals

Reverse Order Studying begins two or three weeks before the test. This method is best illustrated by an example. Assume this schedule:

MONDAY	FINAL 1
TUESDAY	FINAL 2
WEDNESDAY	FINAL 3
THURSDAY	FINAL 4
FRIDAY	FINAL 5

The usual method is to study for final 1 first, followed by finals 2, 3, 4, and 5. The average student studies four to five days before the first final, giving him four to five days for final 1, three to four for final 2, and two to three each for finals 3, 4, and 5. This method requires significant cramming.

Reverse Order Studying requires that you start studying longer in advance and study for final 5 *first*. Then study for 4, followed by 3, 2, and 1.

When you've finished studying, the last final you will have studied for is 1, the first final you'll take! The next-to-last studied for is the second one you'll take, and so forth.

Following this method cuts out pressure and cramming and makes studying much easier.

Survival Strategy #45:
How to Master Take-Home Exams

Reduced-pressure take-home exams are used for three reasons:

1. One class period is not enough time to complete the exam.

2. The material being tested is too complex and may include information (formulas too lengthy to memorize, for example) not worth memorizing but necessary to know for the solution of the problems.

3. The prof is a nonbeliever in tests as an adequate measure of a student's ability.

Take-home exams contain one or two, maybe more, big problems or questions, which call for more research and learning than a test in class can. They take more time to complete and are usually harder, but they are a good learning experience.

The best way to complete a take-home test is to attack the problem(s) according to scientific method:

1. Define the problem.

2. Obtain related data.

3. Form a hypothesis from present knowledge.

4. Test your theory against the data.

5. Form a conclusion.

Repeat steps 3 and 4 if necessary.

If you encounter obstacles, you can discuss them with friends in the class, to get their opinions. But never copy another student's work; it is not only unethical, but profs have an uncanny knack for recognizing assignments that have been plagiarized, no matter how professionally they are disguised.

Survival Strategy #46:
How Exams Are Weighed

Often a prof will announce the value of a quiz, e.g., the first quiz counts for 5 percent of the final grade. Five percent seems negligible, but it isn't. Poor results on a first quiz can cause you to become demoralized and uninterested in the course, and to get negative feelings from the prof and carry over this attitude to other courses.

TREAT EVERY QUIZ AS AN EXAM
AND EVERY EXAM AS A FINAL

Survival Strategy #47:

How Exams Are Graded

Contrary to popular belief, profs are usually fair graders and try to give you the benefit of the doubt. However, the desire to help you decreases as the overall quality of your work decreases. A prof may bend over backward to give you an A when you are short two or three points, but is less inclined to help when the same points are needed to turn a D into a C.

Profs help those who do the work and ignore those who don't. They also place emphasis on improvement.

For objective exams, the prof starts out with a set number of points, usually 100, and deducts for wrong answers. His initial attitude is to deduct as few points as possible. If he sees you may do well (from scanning the test) he will often take off less than if he sees you don't know anything at all.

On the subjective exam, the prof will read several papers and get an idea of the general trend. He gives individual grades based on what he expects and what the group has written.

The claim often made against profs is that they grade on a curve, assuring them that a certain percentage of students will receive each grade. As you can see from the curve on page 85, the largest group will get Cs, then Bs and Ds, and a few As and Fs. This method of grading is beneficial to the prof: an even distribution of grades indicates to the prof's superiors that he is doing a satisfactory job. Too many As would tell them the prof is too lenient; too many Ds and Fs, too hard—or even that he can't teach the subject.

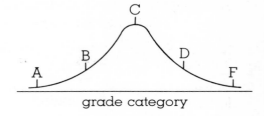

no. of students

grade category

Another method of grading uses a scale, relative to the other students in the class. Say that 90 is the highest grade scored on a test. The range of each grade can be lowered like this:

ORIGINAL SCALE	REVISED SCALE	LETTER GRADE
90–100	84–90	A
80–89	76–83	B
70–79	64–75	C
60–69	50–63	D
0–59	0–49	F

But remember, if you do your work fairness of grading will not make much difference. Good work gets good grades.

Survival Strategy #48:
An Option Called Pass/Fail

Many juniors and seniors get some course credits on a pass or fail basis, which alleviates some pressure.

P/F has its pros and cons. It is a means for students to take a difficult course which otherwise they might not have taken. Study pressure is reduced, enabling the student to concentrate on his area of specialization rather than worry about a required course he's not interested in. Taking a course P/F in your major is not recommended.

The popularity of P/F is limited from the prof's point of view. Students tend to forget about P/F courses, since all they have to do is pass.

Pass/fail courses will not harm a student provided he doesn't take too many, takes none in his major, and doesn't fail!

Survival Strategy # 49:
How to Study for Tests

Here are four methods, adapted from psychology:

1. *Rehearsal during practice:* By rehearsal, or repetition, the material is gone over many times. This increases memory retention.

2. *Overlearning:* After you believe you've mastered the material, continue rehearsing.

3. *Meaningfulness:* The way in which material is learned—by association with other more common words, phrases, or trick sayings—plays an important role in memory. Remember the memory trick with the planets? Make up your own mnemonic devices to aid you in memorizing.

4. *Organization:* Arranging information in groups

of similar characteristics can help you remember related facts.

Questions for exams measure retention in four ways:

1. *Free Recall:* You are to recall straightforward information (completion questions).

2. *Anticipation:* You are to recall items and put them in a sequence (math proofs, computer programs).

3. *Recognition:* You are to recognize words, answers, or phrases in response to a question (multiple choice, matching, true/false).

4. *Relearning:* You are asked the same question in a different part of the exam, or on a later test. Profs tend to repeat questions, especially those the class did poorly on.

NO TRICKS OR SHORTCUTS
WILL HELP YOU IN STUDY

When studying for a test, it is a good idea to test yourself *in writing*. Make up a list of questions about the work, wait a half hour, and then answer them as if you were taking a test. This will force you to write the material again and help you find weak areas.

The Night Before an Exam

RELAX

RELAX

RELAX

The night before an exam is crucial with respect to nervous tension and anxiety. It is important to get a good night's sleep.

It helps you to sleep well if you know you are prepared for the exam. Distraction helps too: watch TV, listen to music, rap—try to forget about the exam. You can review the work lightly, but this is optional. Of course, you can't relax if you've left all the work for the last moment.

Survival Strategy #50:
Why You Should Never Cheat

No professor hates anything more than cheating. Besides insulting the profs on an intellectual level, the cheater insults him on a personal plane. There are four reasons why cheating will hurt you:

1. You'll probably be caught, which can result in an automatic F or even dismissal.

2. Chances are the answers you copy will not all be right. Many profs use two or more tests with different questions or the same questions with varying sequences of numbering. The person next to you or in front of you may be working on an entirely different exam!

3. By cheating, you only hurt yourself. Chances are you will see the material again, probably on the final, where it is impossible to cheat. Then what will you do?

4. You may be able to cheat and get away with

a good grade once, but if you can't do it consistently, what good is cheating?

Pay no attention to your classmates during an exam. They may be sweating it out because they haven't studied. Don't let their frustrated looks affect you.

Survival Strategy #51:
How to Find Out Where You Went Wrong

There are four areas in which you may fall down on an exam:

(1) length of answer;

(2) relevancy, order, proper emphasis of ideas;

(3) accuracy of details;

(4) number of detailed questions answered.

Numbers 1 and 2 usually result from nervousness or your attitude. Numbers 3 and 4 stem from inadequate preparation. You can remedy these before the next exam.

Review the analysis of college testing in this chapter from time to time so that you can take advantage of all the proved methods.

A Personal Note

There you have it: 51 strategies for survival at college. Hundreds of tips, methods, suggestions that have worked for me and thousands of others. Now its up to you . . . and if you've read *The College Survival Kit*, understand it, and apply what's inside, you'll have a great academic career, a super social time, and probably the best four years of your life! Good luck!

ABOUT THE AUTHOR

At 27, IRV BRECHNER is already a self-made man. He runs his own one-man ad agency and is the publisher of *What's New!*, a bi-monthly magazine about retail stores in Essex County, New Jersey, where he lives. A Magna Cum Laude graduate of Seton Hall University, he is taking night courses toward an M.B.A. The creator of the original 6-foot crossword puzzle at 15, Brechner contributes puzzles regularly to various publications.